Secrets of a 6-Figure Real Estate Agent: Blueprint for Rapid Success

Melissa McClendon

Secrets of a 6-Figure Real Estate Agent: Blueprint for Rapid Success

Copyright © 2024 Melissa McClendon.

All rights reserved. In accordance with the U.S. Copyright Act of 1976, the scanning, uploading, and electronic sharing of any part of this book without permission of the publisher constitutes unlawful piracy and theft of the author's intellectual property. If you would like to use material from the book (other than for review purposes), prior written permission must be obtained by contacting the author at Melissa@nolahome.com.

Legacy Builders Publishing
90daylegacybuilders.com

TABLE OF CONTENTS

Introduction	i
Chapter 1: Preparing For Success	1
Chapter 2: Building A Strong Foundation	11
Chapter 3: Prospecting and Lead Generation	25
Chapter 4: Effective Client Acquisition	33
Chapter 5: Successful Listing and Selling Strategies	40
Chapter 6: Continuous Learning and Professional Development	47
Chapter 7: Tracking Progress and Measuring Success	54
Conclusion	58

INTRODUCTION

September 2014, I decided to get my real estate license. I had gone through a divorce and wanted to sell the home I lived in. Since I didn't have enough equity to pay a Realtor, I decided to get a real estate license and sell my home independently. Never could I have imagined that Real Estate would become my career.

In January 2015, my sister was looking to purchase another home. Since I had my real estate license, I offered to assist my sister with her home purchase. I didn't have a clue what I was doing, but my sister was patient with me. We found a home my sister liked, negotiated a sales price, and closed within 30 days.

I received my first commission check from my sister's closing. I earned $4500 for one transaction. At the time, I was a single mom to two daughters. This $4500 gave me an opportunity to pay down some debt and put a lump sum in my savings account. It was such a significant relief to have another source of income. This made me decide that real estate would be my part-time gig to earn some extra money.

My brother-in-law is a contractor. I asked him about any of his contacts that may be involved in real estate. He connected me to two contacts. Both of these contacts allowed me to list their properties. At the end of 2015, I closed 11 transactions for a total of $1.2 million in sales. This sparked my interest in the possibility of doing real estate as a career.

The first time I saw another Real Estate agent's email signature state "Multi-Million Dollar Producer," I was immediately intrigued. What did that mean? And how could

Introduction

I become that since it obviously seemed prestigious? After some research, I decided to have a goal to sell at least $2 million in real estate sales to describe myself as a Multi-Million Dollar Producer. At the end of 2016, I had 35 transactions with over $4 Million in real estate sales as a Part-time Real Estate agent. At the end of 2016, the only option was to quit my full-time and give real estate a full-time effort.

Along the way, I discovered that very few Real Estate agents develop a business earning a 6-figure income. Unknowingly, I created a business that was earning me six figures in less than 2 years. But there were steps and processes that got me there. Every year, production increased. And I learned that the top producers in the industry had a lot in common.

The goal of this book is to teach you the steps, processes, and habits that will help you become a 6-figure income earner. My business is still growing. At the time of writing this book, I'd sold over $80 million in real estate sales. The purpose of providing

Introduction

this information is not to be braggadocious but rather to show that becoming a top producer is not very hard.

If you follow these steps meticulously, you can become a top-producing, six-figure-earning real estate agent. I will go step by step on how I built my career.

CHAPTER ONE

PREPARING FOR SUCCESS

Obtaining Your License

The process of obtaining your Real Estate Salesperson license varies per state. About 90 hours of dedicated classes on national and state license law is usually the first requirement. These classes can be offered by a 3rd party education school or possibly the local real estate board. The training school will require testing to complete the classes and gain a certificate to qualify for the state real estate license test.

Once you receive your certificate verifying that the required training hours are complete, the agent can register for the state and national exams. This is facilitated by a state-certified testing center. Once the agent passes this test, they can apply for their Real Estate license.

One of the requirements with your Real Estate license is to choose a Brokerage within a certain timeframe. This broker will assist with training and managing new Licensees. Usually, the agent has to have a designated commission split with their Broker. As an agent, you want to use a broker who is experienced in training new agents. It is a good idea to interview multiple Brokerages and ask other agents about their experience with their broker.

The new agent will also need to become a member of their local MLS. This will allow access to listings and other valuable information about the local market. This is where agents will input their listings and search for properties for their clients.

Understanding the Real Estate Market

As a new Realtor, you must understand the business you are operating in.

When first starting out, attending Broker's Open Houses is a plus to get to know the market and other movers and shakers in the business. Start by introducing yourself to the agents who have properties listed on the market. You may even offer to treat them to lunch or coffee. If you get to know these top producers in the market, you can start to see their habits and gain insight from them. Also, touring the properties on the market will help you to understand the real estate market. You can learn marketing tools from what other successful agents do to market their listings.

Daily, you should be studying the market updates in your local MLS database. Check what properties are new on the market. See what properties have gone under contract. Check what properties have sold. Start to analyze the market by zip code and area. If you study the market daily, you will develop into an expert. When someone asks you, "How is the market?" You can answer them with knowledge as you will know what areas are more active and what trends are in the market.

There are so many free opportunities for you to learn the market. The local MLS board usually offers free classes and seminars. Many vendors in the industry, such as title companies and lenders offer free information seminars and courses that offer information on your local market. There is no excuse not to educate yourself. The more educated you are as an Agent, the more valuable you become.

Setting Goals... Should an Agent do a Business Plan

Being successful in any business requires a road map. Goal setting is crucial to this road map. If you do not know what you are planning to achieve, how will you know if you are on track?

The most successful people have a "Why" that is bigger than themselves. When I first started in real estate, I wanted to ensure that my daughters had a good education. It was important that my daughter attended a certain school that had a required monthly payment. Initially, this was a major reason for me to do well in real estate. I knew that I had the potential to make enough income to provide for my daughter to attend this school. Throughout my career, my "why" has changed as I have evolved. But my "Why" is always bigger than me. It makes me out of bed when I don't feel like it.

That "Why" will also help to establish goals. It will help you determine how many homes you need to sell and how much income you need to take home. Take some time to yourself and figure out what you want to accomplish.

These are the major goals you need to write down:
- How many homes would you like to sell, or what dollar amount of real estate sales do you plan to hit?
- How many people will you connect with daily, weekly, and monthly?
- How much net income would you like to make?
- What type of client would you like to have?

Write these goals down. Go over them in the morning and at night before bed. Some even write their goals on a whiteboard in their office or as the screen saver on their phone. The more you remind yourself of your goals, the more focused you will become on attaining them.

Your goals should be "SMART" goals. The goals should be Specific, Measurable,

Achievable, Relevant and Time-Bound. Each goal that you write down should meet all of these criteria. Every agent will have different goals depending on their market, circumstances, experiences, and lifestyle.

Once you determine your goals, a business plan should be put into place to reach these goals. For example, if a Real Estate agent wants to sell 20 homes for the year. Reaching this goal will require talking to a certain number of people per week. It usually takes 5 prospecting calls to make one contact, then 10 contacts to make one appointment, and 3 appointments to close one deal. This plan will give you the roadmap to achieving your goals.

Building a Professional Network

One of the first tasks you should begin to do as a new agent is building a Professional Network. This can be done relatively easily and quickly. You can start by attending industry events posted by your local MLS. This will allow an agent to meet Lenders, Title Attorneys, and other industry connections. Often, these vendors are willing to co-market and host knowledge seminars for potential buyers. These vendors can also become a great source of referrals.

At the beginning of your career, you may want to attend as many networking events as possible. Check the calendar for your local Chamber of Commerce, neighborhood association meetings, networking events, and other social gatherings. This allows you to build your database.

When meeting people, start conversations that get the other person talking about their personal lives. Most people enjoy talking about their families and occupations. Most times, you will have an opportunity to let them know that you sell real estate. If you have a digital business card, you can save your contact info to their phone. Or you can give the person your paper business card. Try to gather the person's contact information without being too invasive.

Once you gather a new person's contact information, add them to your database. For years, I used an Excel spreadsheet as my database. Now, I use a more advanced CRM system. In my opinion, as long as you are capturing the lead's information, I believe the program used does not matter so much. You can use Excel or a more advanced CRM to begin to build your professional network. The people in this database are who you will get to know. Remember that people do business with those that they KNOW, LIKE, and TRUST. The more people you know, the more business you will have.

Another important factor in gathering contact information is to learn as much as possible about those in your database. It helps to know their Birthday, Anniversaries, children's birthday and names, and any other pertinent information. This will help you get to know your sphere and provide talking points. You can call on birthdays or even give a $5 gift card for coffee. The more you keep in touch and get to know your contacts, the more they will grow to know and like you. This thoughtfulness will go a long way.

It is imperative to stay in touch with your network. This can be a weekly or monthly newsletter sent by email. A study proved that only 12% of homeowners use the same agent for their next transaction. This is because many agents do not keep in touch with past clients. They lose contact. When it is time for the second transaction, either the client does not remember how to contact the agent, or they form a relationship with another agent. The key is to "stay top of mind" with your network. When they think of real estate, they should think of you.

CHAPTER TWO

BUILDING A STRONG FOUNDATION

Building a Personal Brand and Online Presence

A foundation is what your business stands on. If your foundation is solid and strong, you will always grow your business—one of the first pillars of your foundation in building a personal brand and online presence.

We are in an age where most home-buyers and sellers are getting real estate agent references from social media and online. When searching for a real estate agent, many people search the internet and search for agents in their local area. Without an online presence, many agents are often overlooked.

When I got into the real estate business, Facebook was the biggest social media platform. I made a conscious effort to "friend" as many people that I knew or knew of. This was my way of meeting people virtually and getting my brand out to the masses. By connecting with high school classmates, neighbors, local businesspeople, and politicians, the brand gradually became more and more well-known.

When building a brand, consider the type of client you want to attract. If you plan to sell luxury real estate, your brand should signify luxury. You can easily create a logo on Etsy and Canva. Look for colors and fonts that look more luxurious. Make sure that your attire is sleek and clean. Highlight properties that are considered high-end in your area. When the public thinks of you as an

Agent, your brand should describe you without words.

Another way to create a brand and online presence is by creating an attention-grabbing website. Depending on your budget, you can pay a professional to build a website for you or use simple online website builders such as Wix. The key is to create a website to direct your audience to. Whenever you're posting on social media, direct your audience to your website.

Your online and social media presence must be compelling. Use plenty of images and videos. If you do not have listings of your own yet, ask another agent if you can market their listing.

Make yourself visible in the real estate business by hosting open houses and touring properties. Use this open house opportunity as an avenue to showcase yourself. Do video clips of the property while hosting the open house. Get someone to take some video footage of you interacting with attendees at the open house to use to post on your website and social media platforms. If a Buyer attends the open house and is not represented by an Agent, add them to your database and follow up with them. Even if they do not purchase the home that you hosted the open house on, they can still become a potential client. If a Buyer attends the open house and is represented by an Agent, follow up with their Agent to get feedback and see if the Buyer has further interest. If an Agent attends the open house without a Buyer, follow up with that Agent and thank them for attending it.

Building a Marketing Strategy

The most effective agents are marketing strategists. Marketing is basically promoting yourself to reach buyers and sellers. In order to effectively market, you must reach as many people as possible. But first, you must develop a marketing plan. There are several marketing channels. Top producers have more than one marketing channel that they use consistently.

Decide which platforms you will use to market. I don't recommend trying to master every single platform but rather choosing 2-3 platforms to which you will dedicate your efforts. In my case, I chose to master Instagram, Facebook, and LinkedIn as social media platforms. I plan weekly posts and study the algorithms to reach as many as possible. I plan video and photo content and study the market to provide valuable information to my audience. In your marketing plan, decide which social media platforms you will dominate and how many times you will post per week/month. In my opinion, social media is the most effective (free) way to reach a large audience.

Another marketing channel is targeting certain neighborhoods or farming by using direct mail. This can be done by mailing postcards, door knocking, passing out flyers/door hangers, or cold calling. Direct mail can also include Just Sold/Just Listed postcards, market updates, and invitations to open houses.

I decided that I wanted to sell in the neighborhood that I lived in. I sent out mailers and frequented local restaurants and coffee shops. I even asked if I could leave my business cards and materials at these locations. This allowed me to get my brand out and reach the community. Every month, I did a dedicated mailer to the homeowners in this community. The results did not happen overnight, but eventually, I started to get listings in this community. Also, my brand became known. I would get stopped in different areas by homeowners who received my marketing material. My marketing was working!

Another strategy I used was Advertising to make myself visible to a very large audience. I decided to do a billboard, online magazine, and moving bus campaign. I budgeted for a billboard to be present in different parts of the city for an entire year. I also had a billboard on a public bus. Also, advertising open houses in our local online magazine was effective. This avenue was expensive and may be an option once you get some sales closed.

Other marketing avenues are listed below. Choose what works best for your budget and area. Once you choose, be consistent. The key to your marketing strategy working is being consistent.

- Promotional Items
- Website
- Radio Broadcasts
- Signage
- Name Badges
- Sponsorships

Establishing a Professional Image and Reputation

"Do not leave your reputation to chance or gossip. It is your life's artwork, and you must craft it, hone it, and display it with the craft of an artist." To become a real estate agent with enough business to earn six figures, you must create a professional image and reputation. This is something you build and must be very intentional about.

One thing I always stood on when developing my image was keeping my personal life and opinions to a minimum. It is important to show your audience who you are as a person. I shared photos of my children, hobbies, vacations, etc. However, I was always careful to keep these glimpses into my personal life very tasteful. I never commented on my personal, religious, or political opinions. I created a relatable professional image that only showed glimpses of myself.

One thing that is not discussed enough is your attire. It is important to dress appropriately. To make a statement, a rule of thumb is to always dress a notch above the room. Small pieces such as a nice blazer or classic black pump can make a big difference in how professional you look. At all times, be dressed to impress. You will always run across people who recognize you. Often, if you are dressed nicely, people will ask what you do for a living. Dress to impress!

Have the reputation of being the hardest working Realtor. Go the extra mile as much as possible. Try to anticipate your client's needs and be proactive about fulfilling them. Just getting started 30 minutes to an hour earlier can make a big difference in how much you can get accomplished. Work ethic will get you very far in this business. Be consistent in the type of service you give each client. Deliver on your promises and deadlines. Always be on time for appointments. This will lead to an excellent reputation and repeated referral business.

Be kind to other Realtors and all the people that you come across. Even if you find that you are not a good fit with a client, try your best to maintain a kind attitude. Referring to that client with kindness will keep your reputation positive. Even in difficult times, maintain a positive demeanor. Other Realtors will be excited to work with you if your demeanor is professional and cooperative. I have heard other real estate agents avoid showing a listing or accepting an offer from an Agent who has a reputation for being hard to work with or combative.

Building a brand to fit the reputation you want. "Your brand is what people say about you after your name is mentioned when you are not in the room." When others think of you, what comes to mind quickly? Is it professional, luxurious, unique, classy, ethical? A brand is designed. If you want to create an upscale luxury brand, you may not want to advertise that you work with buyers who need credit repair. You will start dressing luxuriously and highlighting luxurious properties on your platforms. Eventually, your brand will be synonymous with luxury and upscale real estate.

Focus on being the expert in your field. Be familiar with the market trends. Create an online and social media presence highlighting your market knowledge. When you are asked, "How is the market?" You will be able to answer intelligently and with expertise. Inform your audience of the latest lending options and interest rates. Constantly learn by staying updated on industry developments, certifications, and further education.

Create a client-focused approach. Anticipate your client's needs and tailor your services to exceed their expectations. Work on having excellent communication skills. If your client calls you first for an update, you have not communicated properly. Be swift with updating your clients on their contracts before they call you for updates. Communicate clearly and don't create false expectations.

Setting up Systems for Organization and Efficiency

The first step in organizing your business is choosing a CRM (Client Relationship Management System). This program is used to capture your client's information. You can track purchase anniversaries, birthdays, and other important dates. Most times, these systems will have automatic features. You can also use this system to send weekly, bi-weekly, or monthly newsletters. I personally use Market Leader. But many other agents use Constant Contact, Monday, or Salesforce. You can do your research to find the CRM that has the best features that you feel will work best for your business.

Implement lead generation tactics to add to the CRM daily. Use a CRM that has nurturing strategies to have multiple touches of clients. This will generate repeat business. Another great lead generation tactic is touching your past clients multiple times per year. You can do this with a newsletter or birthday/anniversary wishes. The Personal Marketing website does multiple touches for you per year for a low cost of around $25.

Managing your files is another important factor to success in your business. Be sure to store all your files for at least 5 years in case you are audited. You can use an online management system such as Skyslope or Google Drive. Or even if you use a paper file, be sure to keep relevant contract information. A transaction coordinator may be a good investment for you. This person will keep track of all relevant contract documents and amendments. They will store the documents and make sure the client has a copy of everything. This is usually a charge of $300-$400 per transaction.

The most successful agents have mastered time management. Organize your time and days. For example, every Monday at 9:00 AM, I start my day and week with my real estate coach. We go through the previous week and set goals for the upcoming week. On Monday at 10 AM, I huddle with my team. We go over our to-do tasks and goals for the week. At 11 AM, I go through all of my listings and update all of the sellers on activity, etc. Each day, I set aside time for lead generation. My appointments usually take place in the afternoon and/or early evening. This allows me the opportunity to organize each day and generate new business.

Setting up systems to organize finances is key for a real estate agent. Taxes are not taken out of commission checks. I would advise consulting with a CPA to help with this process. But even if you are doing it yourself, you must keep track of business expenses. Keep receipts and document all expenses so that you can deduct when you file taxes. It is essential to set about 30% of each commission for taxes. Also, you want to be aware of spending. Needless expenses should be eliminated to increase your profit margin. If you are paying for marketing or services, you want to track your rate of return to determine if these fees are needed.

The keys to success are systems and organization. Have the attitude of constant improvement to pivot if any changes need to be made. These systems will increase productivity and will be your pillar to success.

CHAPTER THREE

PROSPECTING AND LEAD GENERATION

The key to success is in your ability to consistently cultivate potential leads. Prospecting and lead generation are the foundation of a 6-figure real estate agent. In this chapter, we will review techniques to elevate your prospecting game to keep your streams of leads flowing.

Identifying Target Markets and Niches

First, you must understand your local market. Dig deep to analyze trends, demographics, and upcoming changes. This will help you understand the best areas with the highest growth potential.

Define Your Niche

A niche is a specialized segment of the real estate market. This can be luxury properties, first-time homebuyers, commercial real estate, or another specialty. This will allow you to target your marketing and focus on specific clients.

Utilizing Data, Technology and Analytics

You can leverage technology and data analytics to identify potential clients. Your CRM system and local MLS statistics will come in handy with tracking trends and client preferences. You can use these tools to increase your chances of connecting with the right people.

Utilizing Traditional and Digital Marketing Channels

Traditional strategies still play a critical role in marketing. Direct mail and print advertisements still work. Using a combination reaches a broader audience. Real estate signs, flyers, postcards, and brochures are still effective and get your name and branding out to increase visibility.

Digital marketing is the newest wave. In this market, you will need a robust online presence. Creating a social media presence is vital. Having an eye-catching website is also very helpful. Utilize SEO (search engine optimization) to ensure your profile and listings are easily discoverable by potential clients.

You can distinguish yourself as an industry expert by creating digital content. Video is the best way to showcase your expertise. Writing blogs on the local market, real estate tips, and trends can set you apart as the go-to real estate agent. Podcasts and webinars are avenues to make yourself visible and build trust with your audience.

Expanding the Network Through Referrals and Networking

Real estate is a relationship business. It is vital to build relationships through personal connections. Cultivate strong relationships with past clients, colleagues, industry professionals, and anyone you personally do business with. A satisfied client will be one of your most valuable sources of referrals. They will shout your name from the mountaintop and be your biggest commercial. Relationships will lead to a continuous stream of leads.

Client testimonials are a great way to build credibility as a strong real estate agent. Your satisfied clients can provide written or video testimonials. This will encourage other clients to want to work with you. Add these testimonials on your website and social media channels. Your reputation means everything in this business.

As I mentioned earlier, at the beginning of my career, I attended every networking event possible. Attend local events, seminars, and industry conferences to expand your knowledge and network. Build relationships with other professionals, such as mortgage brokers and attorneys. These professionals can be another source of referrals. They can also be a wealth of knowledge to help expand your career. Networking is not just gathering business cards; it is about nurturing genuine connections.

Generating Leads Through Open Houses and Community Events

Open houses are a great way to pick up leads. These leads can be for Sellers or Buyers. If the neighbors see you doing a great job promoting and marketing open houses, they may choose you as their agent when they are ready to list their home. Invite all the neighbors to the open house and get to know them. You also pick up Buyers from open houses. These Buyers may be considering purchasing or actively searching. If the Buyers are not working with an Agent, you can help them with that process. Make sure you market your open houses online and with signs and flyers. Put open house signs with the date and time a few days before the event to capture people's attention. Use social media to promote your open house. You can even advertise a giveaway to entice attendance. Often, you can get an industry vendor to help sponsor food, giveaways, etc.

Follow up promptly with anyone who attends the open house.

Community Involvement

Getting involved in your community will surely bring leads. You can join non-profit organizations, join community groups, and help with charity initiatives. This enhances your connections with people and life satisfaction. But it also allows you to have more visibility with possible clients and builds your reputation as a trustworthy agent.

Showcase Local Businesses

Form partnerships with local businesses: frequent local coffee shops and restaurants. Post pictures online and make reviews of these places. The local businesses will appreciate the support. Often, these businesses will cross-promote. Supporting these businesses can lead to mutual referrals and expand your reach in the community.

In conclusion, consistent prospecting and lead generation require a combination of traditional and digital strategies, a deep understanding of the target market, and a commitment to building meaningful relationships. When these methods are implemented, you will be on your way to becoming a 6-figure real estate agent.

CHAPTER FOUR

EFFECTIVE CLIENT ACQUISITION

To become a 6-figure real estate agent, you must master client acquisition. In this chapter, we will discuss the strategies and skills needed to build a client database and convert these clients to long-term, repeat clients. These skills range from effective communication and building trust to negotiation skills and providing exceptional customer service. Let's delve into these skills.

Mastering the Art of Effective Communication and Negotiation

Clear communication is one of the pillars of being an effective real estate agent. Learn how to speak clearly. Communicate being as detail-oriented as possible. Don't assume that your client understands the intricacies of the buying and selling process. Communication builds trust and sets you up for success in negotiation.

Negotiation is a skill that must be mastered in order to succeed in real estate. The focus should be on a win-win for all parties. There is a balance between assertiveness and cooperation.

Building Trust with Clients

Trust begins with building a genuine connection. Learn how to interact authentically, which will build a relationship that will go beyond the transaction. Building relationships will create repeat clients and multiple referrals.

Listening is so important in communication. If you really take the time to listen effectively, you will understand your client's needs and wants. Develop empathy by placing yourself in the client's position so that you can have compassion for their emotions. This level of understanding and patience will be greatly appreciated. Having a positive experience during such an important transaction will make your clients become raving fans.

Being transparent builds trust, giving your clients all the facts and sharing information even if the conversation is not the easiest. ALWAYS set realistic expectations. Sometimes, clients will be disappointed with agents when expectations should have been set from the beginning. This would have removed false hope. This may mean that you may not gain a client. But I would rather be realistic than give false hope to an angry client later.

ALWAYS set a high ethical bar. Be professional at all times, even when other parties are acting unprofessional. Keep your emotions in check. Carrying yourself as an emotionally intelligent professional will become your most valuable asset in this industry. I've seen so many agents behave negatively, which ruins their reputation among colleagues and clients. Build a trustworthy, professional reputation.

Investigate The Client's Needs

It is essential to do client interviews when you start working with someone new. This can be informal. But there needs to be a set of questions; you get answers from each client. These questions will vary depending on what type of client you are working with. For example, if you are taking on a new buyer, the questions may look like this:

- How many bedrooms and bathrooms are needed? Is there a minimum square footage?

- Are you pre-approved, or do you need help getting financing in order?
- What area would you like to live in?
- What are your MUST haves?
- What can you compromise on?
- Do you need any concessions from the seller, such as closing cost assistance?
- What price range are you looking in?

These questions will help with providing personalized and satisfactory service. Determine what questions you will ask each client during your first meeting. You can probably create a checklist document that you can provide to the client to fill out or ask in person. This will help you tailor your plan to your client's needs.

Every client is different. So, tailor your services to your client's specific needs. Develop the ability to listen to your client's needs to know how to pivot for each client. A first-time homebuyer will need different needs from a seasoned investor.

Exceed Expectations

Exceptional service is the secret to transforming one-time clients into longstanding raving fans. Always aim to exceed your client's expectations. Offer valuable insight, comps before requested, give frequent updates, etc. Go the extra mile and watch the impact it has on your business. It is hard to forget those who do such an amazing job. Your clients will rant and rave about their experience working with you.

Build Life-Long Relationships

Longevity in the real estate business is built on long-term relationships. You have to develop strategies to stay top of mind and keep in contact with clients. You will have repeat business, and your clients will refer you out often.

Becoming a successful real estate agent is a lot more than closing deals. It is about building relationships that last a lifetime. By mastering communication, building trust, conducting research and analysis, and providing exceptional service, you will lay the foundation for a six-figure success story in the competitive real estate field.

CHAPTER FIVE

SUCCESSFUL LISTING AND SELLING STRATEGIES

In this chapter, we will discuss the significance of creating listing and selling strategies that will create financial success for real estate agents. We are going to discover strategies that will set you apart from your competition.

Pricing Properties Competitively and Strategically

Knowledge is the key. Stay informed on the local and regional markets. Understand the average sales price, days on the market, and list-to-sell ratio. Study this data in different neighborhoods in your local market. As an agent, if you understand your market, you are able to make informed pricing decisions.

Successful agents must be strategic with pricing techniques. The number one goal when representing sellers is to maximize profitability. But the listings must be priced competitively. A balance must be created. Develop the skill to price property in a way that attracts buyers without sacrificing value. Leverage tools such as CMA's and your local MLS to determine accurate prices.

Creating Attention-grabbing Listings and Presentations

When listing a property, establishing a compelling description is key. Create a narrative that describes all of the property's key features. Use exciting verbiage and spotlight the best parts of the property.

The visual presentation of the property is what catches the audience's attention. Use a professional photographer or a high-quality camera. Virtual tours of the property are very effective. Sometimes, extra services such as staging can make a huge difference in the property's presentation. Design a presentation of the listing that makes a lasting impression on clients. Be sure to create a strategy that meets the unique needs of the sellers and the properties.

Hosting Successful Open Houses and Property Showings

The key to open houses is to be strategic about planning and gaining maximum exposure. There are marketing strategies to drive attendance. To begin, start marketing the open house at least a week before the event. Ideally, start marketing 2 weeks in advance by sending postcards and passing out flyers to surrounding homeowners. Let them know that you would like to invite them so they can preview the home—place signs at major intersections a few days before the open house with the address, date, and time.

On the day of the open house, place directional signs near the property pointing to the home. Place an open house sign with balloons in front of the property to draw attention. Make sure the yard is manicured and the home looks inviting for guests to be encouraged to attend.

Advertise the open house on social media at least a week in advance. Create an eye-catching flyer to promote. Usually, I do a paid promotion on Instagram and Facebook for a week until the day of the open house. Creating an Event on Facebook for the open house can also attract interested people.

Another avenue is to promote the open house in your local newspaper. Individually, invite Realtors that you know in case they have clients that may be interested in the property. To gain more exposure, I've created a group tour in the area with other listing agents with properties for sale. There is usually a drawing with a chance to enter if you attend all of the open houses. Each agent participating in the tour can chip in a few dollars to purchase a gift card for $50 or $100. This gift card gives the public more incentive to attend.

Most times, the guests at the open house will not purchase your listing. However, inviting the neighbors will display how you market your listings. It also allows you an opportunity to network with other homeowners. When these neighbors choose to sell their homes, there is a strong possibility you will be chosen as the agent! Enter all the guests that attend your open house into your database to keep in touch with them.

Be creative with your open houses. I've had success with evening open houses to capture those who are working during the day. Offer some light bites or even wine to woo your audience. But open houses are a great opportunity to showcase your marketing talents.

Effective Negotiation Tools to Close Deals

Building strong negotiation skills will help you dominate as a real estate agent. First, understand that negotiation is a collaborative process. The goal is for all parties to win.

The foundation for effective negotiation is building a reputation of trust and credibility with clients and other agents. Negotiation takes active listening. You want to fully understand what goal each party is seeking to reach. Work hard to overcome challenges and obstacles that come up during the transaction.

Stand firm but be willing to bend if needed. Also, communicate your stance in a respectful and professional manner, never responding in anger or arrogance.

Mastering creative marketing strategies for listings and open houses will set you apart from your competition. Strong negotiation skills will guarantee your success for your clients and you.

CHAPTER SIX

CONTINUOUS LEARNING AND PROFESSIONAL DEVELOPMENT
───────────────────────────────

The real estate industry is constantly evolving. In order to stay relevant and at the top of your game, learning and self-development must be at the top of your to-do list. This chapter dives deep into the role of staying abreast of industry trends, attending relevant events, seeking mentorship, and maintaining a growth mindset.

Staying Updated with Industry Trends and Market Insights

To navigate the dynamic real estate market successfully, it is imperative for agents to stay informed about the latest industry trends and market insights. Agents should look at local market trends daily. From new listings to sold listings. This will keep you informed and help steer your clients in the right direction. Also, agents should follow the national real estate trends. This will help with understanding interest rate changes and major changes in the real estate industry. Websites such as Inman follow national trends and are tailored to inform agents and brokers.

Attending Relevant Workshops, Seminars, and Conferences

Face-to-face learning is powerful. Agents are able to expand their knowledge and network with other industry experts. Set a goal to attend at least one seminar or conference per year. The knowledge, connections, and future income potential will more than cover the cost of the event. Tools you can learn at these seminars can help reshape your business approaches. Many times, you will find out about future changes that will be coming down the pipeline in the real estate industry. To become a top producer, you must be ahead of your competition.

Seeking Mentorship and Guidance from Experienced Professionals

Having an experienced mentor or coach is a game changer. I have always had mentors and coaches. Over the years, I have paid hefty prices for coaches who help me implement systems and offer advice on growing my business. To start, seek out other agents that you admire. Offer to assist them for free in exchange for guidance and advice. You will learn a lot about becoming a top producer by being in a company with an experienced top-producing agent. But make sure that you are offering something of value to your mentor. This could mean hosting open houses or helping with showing property, etc. Most top-producing agents are very busy and don't have much time to mentor other agents. But if you provide support, the agent will likely be willing to give time to you in exchange. Look for the mentor and/or coach that you feel comfortable with. This will help your career to grow faster.

Embracing a Growth Mindset

The real estate industry is dynamic and ever-changing. Only those who embrace change will thrive in this business. Always be seeking to grow. Even as an experienced agent, never get the attitude that you know everything. Those who refuse to change and grow usually fade out over time. Those who are constantly elevating will continuously stay at the top.

Overcoming Challenges and Obstacles

Resiliency is the ability to withstand and recover quickly from difficulties. Being a real estate agent comes with many challenges. You are dealing with one of the biggest purchases that most people will experience. This can be an emotional roller coaster with challenges. Top producers are effective with emotional resiliency and the ability to pivot and solve problems. Read books on evolving as a person. The better you become as a person, the better you will be as an agent.

One of the challenges you will face as an Agent is dealing with clients and other agents' personalities. Not all agents have a teamwork attitude. Sometimes, agents can be combative and difficult. As a professional, you must remain emotionally intelligent and stay in control. Even clients can be challenging. Always remain professional and have emotional control. If a client is too challenging for you, referring the client to another agent may be in your best interest.

In negotiations, calmness is your superpower. Having a win-win mentality Is key. Having your client's goal as the target will help keep your emotions in check.

In this business, you must learn to handle rejection. Potential clients may tell you no. They may even decide to work with a different agent. But oftentimes, a no simply means not right now. Clients have told me that they don't want to buy or sell at the moment for different reasons. Only to come back months or even years later and decide to buy or sell. I have even had clients choose to go with another agent for various reasons and return later because they were not pleased. I even have clients who use different agents depending on the property or circumstance. I try not to take it personally because it happens to all of us. However, having the right attitude will allow those clients to feel comfortable to work with you. Always keep a professional demeanor and avoid making business decisions personal. Those people will respect you and may want to work with you in the future.

In conclusion, one of the main characteristics of a 6-figure real estate agent is their constant growth and resilient mindset. These characteristics are developed. Put these tools into action, and you will definitely be on your way!

CHAPTER SEVEN

TRACKING PROGRESS AND MEASURING SUCCESS

Success is not just measured by the number of deals closed. Tracking progress allows you to consistently improve and adapt as needed. It is important to measure key performance indicators, analyze marketing efforts, adjust strategies, and celebrate milestones.

Setting Key Performance Indicators (KPIs) for Tracking Progress

1. Track the number of leads generated from various sources, such as online platforms, referrals, and networking events.

2. Measure the percentage of leads that convert into clients. Understanding conversion rates helps to determine the most effective strategies for turning prospects into closed deals.

3. Average Days on Market. Monitor how long it takes to sell a property. A decreasing Day on the Market indicates effective marketing and sales strategies.

4. Return on Investment (ROI). Evaluate the profitability of marketing campaigns and other business expenses. Track everything from advertising expenses, professional development, and client acquisition. Regularly review the effectiveness of marketing channels. Identify which platforms and campaigns yield the highest

return on investment and allocate resources accordingly.

5. Evaluate the quality of leads from different sources. Focus on channels consistently delivering high-converting leads and consider adjusting or eliminating underpowering sources.

6. Customer Satisfaction. Use surveys and feedback to measure client satisfaction. Happy clients will likely refer new business and help build a positive reputation.

Measuring Success

Always take the time to recognize your achievements and milestones. If you set a goal and you reach it, stop and reflect on it. What did you do to achieve the goal? Really think about it so that you can repeat the process. Identify key factors in your success so that you can create future strategies.

In conclusion, tracking progress and measuring success in real estate is a combination of data-driven analysis, strategic planning, and being committed to continuous improvement. These tools will lay the foundation for success.

CONCLUSION

Being a real estate agent can be a very rewarding, gratifying, and lucrative career. However, it must be run like a business to become a top producer and have longevity. But building a strong foundation, capturing and tracking leads, and staying top of mind with clients will set the stage for your success. As your career flourishes, keeping a strong mindset while tracking your progress will keep you successful for years.

Having a mindset to continually learn and grow will set you apart from the competition. Working on being resilient and calm will make the experience of working with you

Conclusion

better for your clients and other real estate agents.

With these tools for success, you will crush it your first year and for years to come!

Made in the USA
Columbia, SC
01 August 2024